TAMMY J ⌐⌐√

Serial Killers

A Terrifying look at 12 of the most evil True Crime
Stories in America

First edition

This book was professionally typeset on Reedsy.
Find out more at reedsy.com

Contents

1

Introduction

I t is true that every state within this wonderful country of ours has seen its share of evil, pure evil. It, or should I say they, have always been out there.

If you are anything like me, true crime stories flood your news feed and podcasts. We all know the names John Wayne Gacy, Jeffrey Dahmer, Dennis Rader, Gary Ridgway, Ed Kemper, Richard Ramirez and David Berkowitz. Well, maybe you don't know their real names but certainly you have heard of The Killer Clown, the Milwaukee Cannibal, BTK, Lady Killer, the Green River Killer, the Co-ed Killer, the Night Stalker and the Son of Sam.

Podcasts such as Crime Junkies, Serial, and Morbid kept me sane while bunkering down in my home during the Covid 19 pandemic. I, like many of you, turned to podcasts to occupy my time since we couldn't leave our homes. I found myself obsessed with true crime, something I had never had an interest in before. I couldn't wait for the next episode to air and when that didn't happen fast enough I went to their very first episode and listened to every single one of them until I had listened to them all.

I simply could not get enough.

That led me to movies and documentaries and of course books. What fascinates me is how many serial killers I have never even heard of before. They aren't names that are familiar but they are evil just the same. This book is my first, but hopefully not my last. It contains serial killers that may be as new to you as they were to me. Thank you for exploring them with me.

2

Thomas Warren Whisenhant

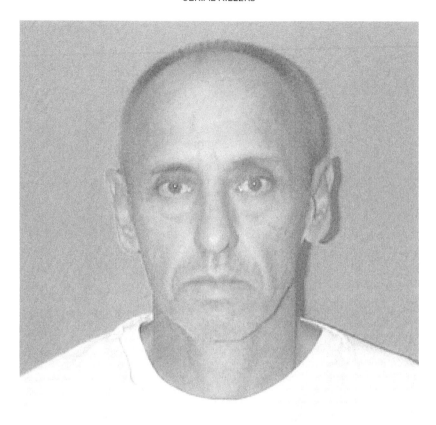

Thomas Warren Whisenhant was born on January 29, 1947 in Prichard, Alabama. At the age of 16, he took his first life, that of 72 year old Lexie Haynes. Whisenhant shot Haynes, the gun was found near his home and the police immediately suspected him of the murder. Unfortunately, he was never charged with Haynes' murder.

Whisenhant joined the United States Air Force where he beat Rose Covington, just 22 years old, with a metal ashtray in the finance office of the Air Force Base. Covington spent two months in the hospital recovering from critical head and facial injuries. Whisenhant was convicted of assault with intent to commit murder on March 14, 1966. On November 28, 1973, Whisenhant was granted parole.

It didn't take long before Whisenhant was at it again, this time focusing on convenience store clerks. On November, 21, 1975, Whisenhant beat and shot 28 year old Patricia Hitt. On March 16, 1976, he kidnapped and murdered 44 year old Venora Hyatt. This time, Whisenhant returned to where he had left Hyatt's body, stole her watch to give to his wife and mutilated her body. On October 16, 1976, Whisenhant abducted 23 year old Cheryl Lynn Payton. Payton was kidnapped and driven to a wooded area, where Whisenhant raped her and shot her in the head. Once again, Whisenhant returned to the scene the next day and mutilated her body.

Fortunately, Whisenhant was spotted in the woods and was brought to justice. Little did the police know just how evil he was, it was then that Whisenhant confessed to the murders of Hitt and Hyatt. Some time later, he confessed to the murder of Haynes when he was just a teenager. On August 9, 1977, Whisenhant was sentenced to death after a capital murder verdict. This sentence was reversed and he had a new trial in 1981. After many appeals and almost 33 years on death row, Thomas Warren Whisenhant was executed on May 27, 2010.

3

The Butcher Baker - Robert Christian Hansen

Robert Christian Hansen was born on February 15, 1939 in Estherville, Iowa. As a child, he was described as being shy, a bit of a loner without many friends. He struggled to get the attention of the girls in high school and turned to hunting and archery to fill his time.

On December 7, 1960, Hansen was arrested for burning down the Board of Education Bus Garage. He was sentenced to three years but only served twenty months before being released. He spent additional time in jail over the next few years for petty theft.

In 1967, Hansen moved to Alaska, settling in Anchorage. Here, he broke several local hunting records and seemed to be well liked. He stayed out of trouble for several years. In December 1971 he was arrested not once but twice. Once for the abduction and attempted rape of a housewife and once for raping a sex worker. In a plea bargain, he pled no contest to assault with a deadly weapon for the attack on the housewife in exchange the rape charge against the sex worker was dropped. Hansen was sentenced to 5 years but served only 6 months before being placed in a halfway house.

According to Hansen, he began murdering in the early 1970s. He started with young Alaskan women aged 16 - 19 but soon the profile of his victims changed to sex workers. Hansen would pick them up, rape them, fly them to a secluded area in his plane and then hunt them like animals before killing them. The exact number of women is unknown but it is believed that he raped and assaulted thirty women, killing at least 17 of them.

Hansen was caught after the brave actions of 17 year old Cindy Paulson. Hansen kidnapped and raped Paulson on June 13, 1983 and drove her to his plane. While he was busy preparing the plane, Paulson escaped but left her sneaker in his car so that the police would have evidence that she was there. It took several months, but on October 27, 1983, police searched Hansen's home and found a map they believe indicated where he buried his victims along with trophies of his victims that he kept.

Hansen eventually confessed to 17 murders and led police to 17 grave sites, 12 of which the authorities had not yet found. Hansen was formally charged with only 4 of these murders along with the kidnapping and rape of Paulson. He was sentenced to 461 years in prison without the possibility of parole. Hansen died on August 21, 2014.

4

Maryvale Serial Shooter - Aaron Juan Saucedo

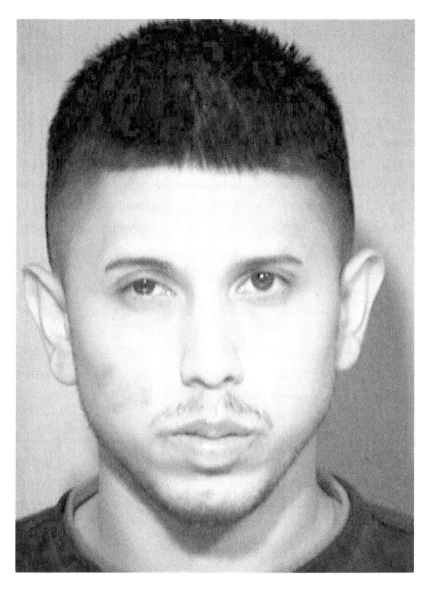

B orn April 6, 1994, Aaron Juan Saucedo was described as a sweet and friendly child. Somehow this sweet and friendly child grew up to be a complete monster with no regard for human life.

It should be noted that as of this writing, Saucedo has not been convicted of any of these crimes. He pled not guilty on July 6, 2017 and is awaiting trial which is currently scheduled for early 2024.

His shooting rampage is said to have begun on August 16, 2015 with the murder of his mother's boyfriend, 61 year old Raul Romero, while he was standing in his own driveway. He then started the new year off by killing 22 year old Jesse Olivas on January 1, 2016. On March 17, 2016 he shot and wounded a 16 year old boy and threatened to do the same to a 17 year old boy. The very next day, he shot and wounded 21 year old Michael Aldama.

At this point people could not feel safe, the shootings were happening all around Maryvale, some were drive-by shootings, some happened while the victims were driving, others when they were walking. The shootings continued on April 1, 2016 with the death of 21 year old Diego Verdugo-Sanchez and again on April 19, 2016 resulting in the death of 55 year old Krystal Annette White.

In June 2016, 5 additional lives were taken, 32 year old Horacio Peno was killed on June 3; 19 year old Manuel Castro Garcia on June 10; and 33 year old Stefanie Ellis, her 12 year old daughter Maleah and her 31 year old friend Angela Linner on June 12.

Arnol Castillo Rojas, 21, and a 4 year old boy were shot at while driving but fortunately neither of them were injured. Rojas later was able to pick Saucedo from a police lineup on April 22, 2017. On May 8, 2017, Saucedo was arraigned for the murder of Raul Romero. An additional 8 counts of first degree murder were added on June 30, 2017 along with other charges including, attempted murder, drive by shooting, aggravated assault, endangerment and discharging a firearm at a structure. As stated earlier, Saucedo pled not guilty to all charges and is still awaiting trial.

5

The Phantom Killer

B oth Arkansas and Texas were terrorized during 1946 when an unknown man took the lives of 5 people. These murders are sometimes referred to as the Moonlight Murders.

On February 22, 1946, 25 year old Jimmy Hollis and 19 year old Mary Jean Larey were attacked while parked. Both were beaten but both survived. Hollis & Larey described their attacker as a man with a white mask with eye holes cut out and said he was 6 foot tall. The rest of their descriptions did not match.

On March 24, 1946, just one month later this Phantom Killer struck again, this time he killed 29 year old Richard Griffin and 17 year old Polly Ann Moore, shooting them both in the back of the head and posing their bodies inside their vehicle.

On April 14, 1946, Paul Martin, just 17 years old and 15 year old Betty Jo Booker were found murdered after Martin picked Booker up after a musical performance. Martin's vehicle was found with the keys still in the ignition, his body was found over a mile away and Booker's body was found about 3 miles away from the vehicle. It is reported that these two teenagers gave the Phantom Killer a fight. In the end, Martin was shot 4 times and Booker was shot twice.

Although some do not believe this next case is related, others believe it is the work of the Phantom Killer. On May 3, 1946, 37 year old Virgil Starks was shot twice through a window in his home. His wife, Katy Starks, 36, heard the noise and upon finding her husband reached for the phone to call police. This is when she was shot twice through that same window. Miraculously, she was able to run to a neighbor's house for help and survived.

Although many suspects were brought in and interviewed, no one has been charged with these murders.

6

Rodney Alcala - The Dating Game Killer

R odney Alcala was born Rodrigo Jacques Alcala-Buquor on
August 23, 1943 in San Antonio Texas. He later relocated to Los
Angeles with his mother. At the age of 17 he joined the Army
but after receiving an antisocial personality disorder diagnosis he was
discharged in 1964. Alcala graduated from UCLA with a degree in fine
arts in 1964.

In 1968, Alcala attacked an 8 year old girl, Tali Shapiro. He fled to New Hampshire and began using the name John Berger. After being recognized he was arrested, pled to child molestation and served just 34 months.

On July 24, 1979, Alcala was arrested for the abduction and murder of 12 year old Robin Samsoe in Huntington Beach, California. He was convicted in 1980 but that conviction was overturned in 1984. He was tried again in 1986 and was found guilty again, however this conviction was again overturned in 2001.

Fortunately, while he sat in prison waiting for another trial, advances in DNA evidence allowed law enforcement to tie him to additional crimes. When he was retried in 2010 it was not only for the murder of Samsoe but also for 18 year old Jill Barcomb, 27 year old Georgia Wixted, 32 year old Charlotte Lamb, and 21 year old Jill Parenteau. In February 2010, Alcala was found guilty of all 5 murders and sentenced to death.

In 2012, Alcala pled guilty to the deaths of Cornelia Crilley & Ellen Hoover, in New York City, both just 23 years old. Crilley was killed in her apartment in June of 1971 where she was raped and strangled. Hoover disappeared on June 15, 1977 and her remains were discovered in Westchester County in 1978. On Hoover's calendar was an entry showing a meeting with John Berger on the day she disappeared. He was sentenced to 25 years to life for this conviction.

In 2016, Alcala was also charged with the 1977 murder of Christine Ruth Thornton in Wyoming. Wyoming officials did not extradite Alcala. Alcala died on July 24, 2021 in prison while awaiting execution.

Alcala received the nickname the Dating Game Killer, because he appeared on the television show in September of 1978 where he claimed to be a professional photographer and came across as charming. As bachelor #1 on The Dating Game, he was chosen by Cheryl Bradshaw but after meeting him in person, Bradshaw chose not to go out with him. This decision may very well have saved her life.

7

Michael Bruce Ross

B orn in Putnam, Connecticut on July 26, 1959, Micahel Bruce
Ross was described as being antisocial in his youth. He was
an outstanding student in high school and attended Cornell
University in Ithaca, New York where he graduated in May of 1981 with a
degree in economics.

Ross raped and murdered in both Connecticut and New York between 1981 - 1984. He confessed to 8 murders; 25 year old Dzung Ngoc Tu on May 12, 1981; 17 year old Tammy Williams on January 5, 1982; 16 year old Paula Perrera in March 1982; 23 year old Debra Smith Taylor on June 15, 1982; 19 year old Robin Dawn Stavinsky on October 23, 1983; 14 year olds April Brunais & Leslie Shelley on April 22, 1984; and 17 year old Wendy Baribeault on June 13, 1984.

Ross pled guilty to the murders of Taylor & Williams in July 1987; he received a sentence of 120 years. Later he was tried for the murders of Baribeault, Brunais, Shelly & Stravinsky. He received 2 life sentences and 6 death sentences. In July 1994, the Connecticut State Supreme Court held up his convictions but overturned the death penalty. In 1998, Ross was pleading to be executed but later changed his mind. On April 6, 2000 he was once again given the death penalty. On September 24, 2001, Ross pled guilty to the murder of Perrera. He was not brought to trial on the murder of Ngoc Tu. He spent 18 years on death row and died by lethal injection on May 13, 2005.

8

Steven Brian Pennell - The Route 40 Killer

S teven Brian Pennell was born in Glasgow, Delaware on November 22, 1957. His childhood is said to have been unremarkable, living with both his parents throughout. He was a good student. He was an electrician, was married and had two children.

On November 29, 1987, 23 year old nurse, Shirley Ellis, was delivering a meal to a sick patient when she made the mistake of accepting a ride from Pennell. Her mutilated body was found just a short time later. Her hands were tied to her feet and she was attacked with a hammer to her head.

On June 28, 1988, a 31 year old sex worker, Catherine DiMauro's body was found naked and tortured. Her hands were tied to her feet and she too, was attacked with a hammer to the head.

On August 22, 1988, 28 year old sex worker, Margaret Lynn Finner disappeared. Witnesses reported seeing her get into a blue Ford van. Her body was found 3 months later in the Chesapeake-Delaware Canal.

September 14, 1988, Renee Taschner, an undercover police officer posing as a prostitute saw a blue van drive by several times in a short time frame. She moved to a more deserted area in hopes that the van would stop. Her plan worked and Pennell stopped, opened the back door to the van and tried to get Taschner to get it. Taschner refused to get inside the van but was able to pull fibers from the blue carpeting in the van and got the license plate which traced back to Pennell.

On September 20, 1988, the body of 22 year old sex worker, Michelle Gordon was found tortured at the Chesapeake-Delaware Canal. Then just a few days later, September 23, 1988, Kathleen Anne Meyer disappeared. She was last seen by a police officer, getting into a blue van. The police officer noted the license plate. She was never seen again.

After obtaining a search warrant for Pennell's van, the police connected the blue fibers found on the victims to the fibers in the van. They also found blood and hair of the victims along with whips, handcuffs, restraints, needles, knives and pliers. On November 29, 1988 he was arrested. On November 23, 1989, Pennell was convicted of the murders of Ellis & DiMauro. He was sentenced to 2 life sentences, not the death penalty. He was later convicted of the murders of Gordon & Meyer.

Pennell fired his attorney and defended himself, asking for the death penalty. Delaware law required a second hearing which was held on October 31, 1991. On March 14, 1992 Pennell was executed by lethal injection.

9

Aileen Wuornos

A ileen Wuornos was born in Rochester, Michigan on February 29, 1956. Her childhood was extremely difficult. She never met her father, who was serving time for child molestation when he committed suicide. Her mother abandoned her and her brother. She moved in with her grandmother who was an alcoholic and later died of a liver disease, and her grandfather, who was known to be very violent.

Wuomos claims that her grandfather sexually abused her as a child and that she had a sexual relationship with her brother. She was forced out of the home by her grandfather after having given up a baby boy for adoption. She grew up supporting herself by being a sex worker and moved to Florida where she had many run-ins with the authorities.

During her reign of terror, Wuomos shot and killed 6 men. Richard Mallory, age 51, was her first kill. David Andrew Spears, age 47, went missing May 19, 1990. Spears was found on June 1, 1990; he had been shot 6 times. 40 year old Charles Edmund Carskaddon was murdered on May 31, 1990. His body was found on June 6, 1990; he had been shot 9 times. 65 year old Peter Abraham Siems was presumed dead after Wuomas was seen abandoning Siem's car and her palm print was found on the door handle. His body was never found. Troy Eugene Burress, age 50, went missing on July 31, 1990. Burress' body was found on August 4, 1990; he was shot twice. 56 year old Charles Richard Humphreys was murdered on September 11, 1990. His body was found the next day; he was shot 7 times. The body of Walter Jeno Antonio, age 62, was found on November 19, 1990; he was shot 4 times.

On January 27, 1992, Wuomos was found guilty of first degree murder of Mallory and received the death penalty. She later pled guilty to the other 5 murders, receiving a death sentence for each of them. She was executed on October 9, 2002 at the Florida, Broward Correctional Institution.

10

Paul Durousseau

P aul Durousseau was born in Beaumont, Texas on August 11, 1970. He moved to Los Angeles, California as a child. Durousseau joined the Army in 1992 and was stationed in Germany. It was there that he met his wife. In 1996, they were assigned to Ft. Benning, Georgia. This is when his troubles really began.

In 1997, he was charged with the kidnapping and rape of a young woman but was acquitted. He was later court-martialed and received a dishonorable discharge in 1999 in connection with stolen property.

On September 7, 1997, the body of 26 year old Tracy Habersham was found. She was strangled. Durousseau was a suspect in this murder but not enough evidence connected him to the crime.

Durousseau, his wife and two daughters moved to Jacksonville, Florida. In 1999, Durousseau was seen leaving an apartment carrying a television set. This apartment belonged to 24 year old Tyresa Mack who was found in the apartment having been raped and killed.

In June 2001, Durousseau was charged with sexual assault of a woman in Jacksonville. He was convicted and sentenced to 30 days in jail and 2 years probation. Later that same year, he served 1 ½ months for physically assaulting his wife.

On December 19, 2002, 18 year old Nicole Williams was found in a ditch. Williams was wrapped in a blanket; she was raped and strangled to death. Just a few weeks later, 19 year old Nikia Kilpatrick was found dead in her apartment. Kilpatrick had been raped and strangled; she was 6 months pregnant at the time. Kilpatrick had two young boys who were in the apartment when she was found by family members on January 1, 2003; one was just 2 years old and the other was 11 months old. Neither child was injured in the attack.

On January 10, 2003, 20 year old Shawanda Denise McCalister was found in her apartment. McCalister was pregnant at the time of the murder, she too, had been raped and strangled.

A construction crew discovered the body of 17 year old Jovanna Jefferson in a ditch on February 5, 2003. Police responding to the call discovered the body of 19 year old Surita Cohen just 6 feet away; she had been reported missing on February 4, 2003. Both victims had been seen with a cab driver. This lead, along with a lead that Jefferson's mom had provided, pointed to Durousseau, a local cab driver. DNA evidence linked Williams, Kilpatrick and McCalister.

On February 6, 2003, Durousseau was arrested on a violation of probation. This allowed law enforcement time to build a case against him for the murders. On June 17, 2003, Durousseau was charged with 5 counts of first degree murder. On December 13, 2007, Durousseau was sentenced to death. The death sentence was overturned in 2017 and Durousseau was sentenced to life without the possibility of parole on December 10, 2021.

Durousseau is currently serving out his sentence at the Walton Correctional Institution.

11

The Honolulu Strangler

The Honolulu Strangler terrorized this peaceful area throughout 1985 and 1986. Vicky Purdy, a 25 year old married woman was reported missing by her husband on May 29, 1985 after she failed to return home after going out with friends. Purdy's body was found in the Keehi Lagoon. The case went cold quickly as there were no clues or leads.

On January 14, 1986, 17 year old Regina Sakamoto missed her school bus. She phoned her boyfriend to let him know that she was taking the public bus and would be late getting to school. She was last seen waiting for that bus. Sakamoto's body was also found at Keehi Lagoon close to where Purdy's body had been found.

Just two weeks later, the body of 21 year old Denise Hughes was found in a drainage canal near where Purdy & Sakamoto were found. Hughes took the bus to work. 24 year old Louise Madeiros was reported missing on March 26, 1986. Madeiros had returned home from a trip visiting family; she was 3 months pregnant. She was last seen at the Honolulu airport bus stop. Her body was found under a freeway overpass with the same injuries as Purdy, Sakamoto and Hughes.

Liada Pesce, 36, was reported missing on April 29, 1986. Her car was found on the side of the highway. Witnesses reported seeing a white man and a van near her car. Pesce's body was found on Sand Island after police received a tip and were led to Sand Island by 43 year old Howard Gay. Gay told the police that a psychic had told him where to find Pesce. Pesce's body had the same injuries as the other victims.

Gay was arrested for Pesce's murder on May 9, 1986. During the interrogation he maintained his innocence and was later released. No other murders were ever linked to these. Gay died in 2003 without being charged with the murders.

12

David Edward Maust

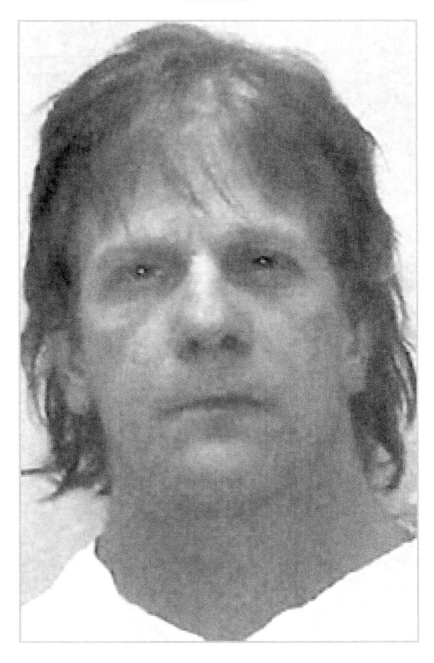

D avid Edward Maust was born in Connellsville, Pennsylvania on April 5, 1954. He moved to Chicago, Illinois with his family, but his father soon left. Maust's childhood showed some disturbing behavior including the killing of a squirrel with a baseball bat.

Maust's mother turned to the court for help when he was only 9 years old; he was committed to Cook County Sanitarium for 4 years. While at the sanitarium, doctors described Maust as bright and had a knack for remembering sports statistics. Staff, both doctors and nurses, all agreed that Maust was not mentally ill. Even so, his mother refused to have him return home. Some theorize that this is because he looked very much like his father.

He was transferred to Children's Home when he was 13, he was only blocks from his family home at this time. While there, at age 15 Maust choked a boy while they were playing. He also used a rope to strangle another boy . Both times he stopped himself and apologized before causing serious injury.

When he was 17, Maust ran away from the Children's Home and went to his family house. His mother, not wanting him around, insisted that he join the Army. So he did. Maust was stationed in Frankfort, Germany.

In 1974, 13 year old James McClister went for a ride with Maust. Maust drove him to the forest, tied him to a tree and beat him. Although there were no witnesses, Maust was court-martialed for McClister's death and was sentenced to 3 years in Leavenworth, a federal prison in Kansas. Maust was released in 1977.

In 1977, Maust stabbed a friend who was asleep on his couch in his Chicago, Illinois apartment. The friend survived the attack. Maust was found not guilty at trial. In 1981, after looking for someone from the Children's Home and coming up empty handed, Maust picked up 15 year old Donald Jones. Jones was stabbed and was drowned.

At this time, Maust moved to Texas. Here he stabbed a 14 year old teenager that he had coaxed to a local motel. Maust was arrested and received a sentence of 5 years. While serving this sentence, in 1982, Maust was extradited back to Illinois for the murder of Jones.

Maust was found unfit to be tried for this murder and spent many years in mental health facilities. In 1994, Maust pled guilty for Jone's murder and was sentenced to 35 years. Unfortunately, he was credited with time served and time for good behavior which led to his release in 1999. Maust almost begged not to be released, he wrote a 5 page letter to the Department of Corrections but having no reason to hold him, he was released.

In 2001, Maust got into trouble again when he hit an acquaintance with a metal pipe. The individual reported the assault but did not want to prosecute.

On December 12, 2003, Maust was arrested for strangling 16 year old James Raganyi after Raganyi's body was found encased in concrete in the basement of Maust's Hammond, Indiana home. Also found wrapped in plastic and encased in concrete were 13 year old Michael Dennis and 19 year old Nick James.

In November 2005, Maust pled guilty to 3 counts of first degree murder and received 3 life sentences. Maust hung himself in his prison cell on January 20, 2006.

13

Richard Grissom

B orn November 10, 1960 in South Korea, Richard Grissom is the son of a US Army Sergeant. He lived in Leavenworth Kansas. Grissom was well liked, popular in high school, intelligent and even played on the football team.

At the age of 16, Grissom beat his 72 year old neighbor, Hazel Meeker to death. He was apprehended a short time later and was convicted in April 1977 in juvenile court. He was sentenced to the Boys Industrial Center in Topeka, Kansas. Grissom along with a couple of other boys escaped in February 1979 but were recaptured quickly. He was released in 1980.

June 18, 1989, 24 year old Marie Butler of Overland Park Kansas disappeared after visiting a friend. She was reported missing the next day when she did not show up to work. Butler's car was found in an apartment complex on June 25 and witnesses reported seeing a man running away from the car.

22 year old roommates Theresa Brown and Christine Rusch threw a farewell party for Brown as she was moving out of the apartment. Neither of them showed up for work the next day and were reported missing. Witnesses placed Grissom at the farewell party.

Grissom was seen using Brown's bank card on a surveillance video. His car and storage lockers were searched. Both Brown's and Rusch's bank cards were found. Hairs collected were tested against the girls' brushes and were found to be a probable match. Pubic hairs collected from the girls' apartment were tested and found to be a match to Grissom.

Grissom was located in Corpus Christi, Texas where he was arrested. As of this writing, Grissom is serving his sentence at El Dorado Correctional Facility and will be eligible for parole in 2093. Grissom has not revealed where the bodies are and they have never been found.

14

Conclusion

The research into these 12 serial killers leaves me in disbelief. Time and time again, these animals were in our prison systems just to be released. Many of these victims could have been saved had the evil remained in prison instead of being released to the unsuspecting public; but that debate is for another time.

By the numbers...these 12 serial killers murdered more than 75 people when you include the two unborn babies of 2 of the victims. They injured in one way or another an additional 30 plus people. The survivors will continue to suffer throughout their entire lives, this is trauma that is not easily forgotten. These 12 are just a small sampling of the evil that walks our streets. 7 of the 12 are dead, 2 are unknown, 2 are serving out their sentence and 1 is still awaiting his trial.

To the families of the many victims, I am truly sorry for your loss and suffering. I hope that these true crime stories you have just read have enlightened you in some way. If I could ask just one small favor, please leave a review on Amazon and watch for more of my books coming soon.

15

References

Wikipedia contributors. (2023). Thomas Whisenhant. *Wikipedia.* https://en.wikipedia.org/wiki/Thomas_Whisenhant

Wikipedia contributors. (2023b). Robert Hansen. *Wikipedia.* https://en.wikipedia.org/wiki/Robert_Hansen

Wikipedia contributors. (2023a). Aaron Saucedo. *Wikipedia.* https://en.wikipedia.org/wiki/Aaron_Saucedo

DiRienzo, D. (2022). This Disturbing Murder Spree In Arkansas Is So Creepy It Inspired A Movie. *OnlyInYourState®.* https://www.onlyinyourstate.com/arkansas/murder-spree-so-creepy-it-inspired-movie-ar/

Wikipedia contributors. (2023b). Texarkana Moonlight Murders. *Wikipedia.* https://en.wikipedia.org/wiki/Texarkana_Moonlight_Murders

Rodney Alcala. (2023, April 27). *Biography.* https://www.biography.com/crime/rodney-alcala

Anthony, M. (2023). Male Serial Killer Michael Bruce Ross (The Roadside Strangler). *HellHorror.* https://hellhorror.com/serial-killers/michael-bruce-ross-serial-killer-77.html

Bell, R. (n.d.). *Michael Bruce Ross: Staring Death in the Face — Paula*

Perrera — Crime Library. https://crimelibrary.org/serial_killers/predato rs/michael_ross/index.html

Crime Busters. (2020, December 11). *Steven Brian Pennell - The Route 40 Killer* [Video]. YouTube. https://www.youtube.com/watch?v=Cdhk7q iTgoE

Aileen Wuornos. (2023, April 27). *Biography.* https://www.biography. com/crime/aileen-wuornos

Paul Durousseau - Bing video. (n.d.). https://www.bing.com/videos/riv erview/relatedvideo?q=Paul+Durousseau&mid=4FAF74AB35177A64527 44FAF74AB35177A645274

Wikipedia contributors. (2023a). Paul Durousseau. *Wikipedia.* https://en.wikipedia.org/wiki/Paul_Durousseau

Goodwin, L. (2021). The tragic deaths of five women and an escaped murderer known as the "Honolulu Strangler." *BYUH Ke Alaka'i.* https://k ealakai.byuh.edu/the-tragic-deaths-of-five-women-and-an-escaped-murderer-known-as-the-honolulu-strangler

Wikipedia contributors. (2023d). Honolulu Strangler. *Wikipedia.* https://en.wikipedia.org/wiki/Honolulu_Strangler

Wikipedia contributors. (2023e). David Edward Maust. *Wikipedia.* https://en.wikipedia.org/wiki/David_Edward_Maust

SERIAL KILLER, DAVID MAUST. (n.d.). SERIAL KILLER CALENDAR - SERIAL KILLER TRADING CARDS- SERIAL KILLER MAGAZINE - SERIAL KILLER DVDS - Murderabelia, Serial Killer Calendar Nicolas Claux James Gilks. https://serialkillercalendar.com/SERIAL-KILLER-DAVID-MAUS T.php

Printed in Great Britain
by Amazon